Revolutions Around The World

Master Tim Yerik

Made with ❤ on the Notion Press Platform

www.notionpress.com

Dedication

I dedicate this book to God the Almighty, who gives me strength every day. To my parents, who always support and encourage me. To my teachers, who guide me with knowledge and wisdom. And to my friends, who bring joy and laughter into my life.

Contents

Preface

History is full of moments when people stood up to make their voices heard. Revolutions are some of the most important examples of this. In this book, I explore three major revolutions: the American, French, and Russian revolutions. Each one of these events changed the course of history, and I wanted to understand more about why they happened and what they achieved.

The American Revolution showed how a group of colonies fought for their independence and built a new nation. The French Revolution was a powerful uprising against the monarchy and introduced new ideas about freedom and equality. The Russian Revolution brought about one of the biggest political changes in modern history, leading to the rise of the Soviet Union. Each of these revolutions had different goals, but they all shared a common desire for change.

Through this book, I hope to explain these events in a way that is easy to understand. I have organized the revolutions in the order they happened, so you can see how history unfolded. I believe that by learning about the past, we can better understand the present and make decisions that will shape a better future.

-Tim Yerik

Acknowledgments

Writing this book has been a challenging yet rewarding experience, and I could not have done it without the support of many important people in my life. First, I want to thank my parents. They have always believed in me and have given me the encouragement I needed to follow my dreams, including writing this book. Their love and guidance mean everything to me.

I would also like to express my gratitude to my teachers. Their dedication to teaching has inspired me to learn more about the world around me, especially history. They have shown me the importance of understanding past events and how they connect to the present. Without their lessons, I wouldn't have developed the interest and knowledge that led me to write this book.

Lastly, I want to thank my friends for their constant support and kindness. Whether through listening to my ideas or encouraging me to keep going, they have helped me stay motivated. Their friendship is something I deeply appreciate, and I am grateful to have them by my side throughout this journey.

-Tim Yerik

This book is going to talk about *major revolutions* that happened in history in a chronological order

1. The American Revolution

After the discovery of "the new world", many European countries tried to colonise the Americas. The countries that took part in this are Britain, France and Spain. The British after about a century of warring with native tribes and other European powers it established some colonies in the Americas and so did other European powers. After some disputes with the French about a French fort, Fort Duqesne in disputed territory, the British sent a Liteunant Colonel named George Washington with a combined force of British and Native Americans to go and capture the fort.

Portrait of George Washington

This battle was known as *the battle of fort Necessity* long story short, this battle led to a major global confilct known as the seven years war which included many European powers taking part in it.

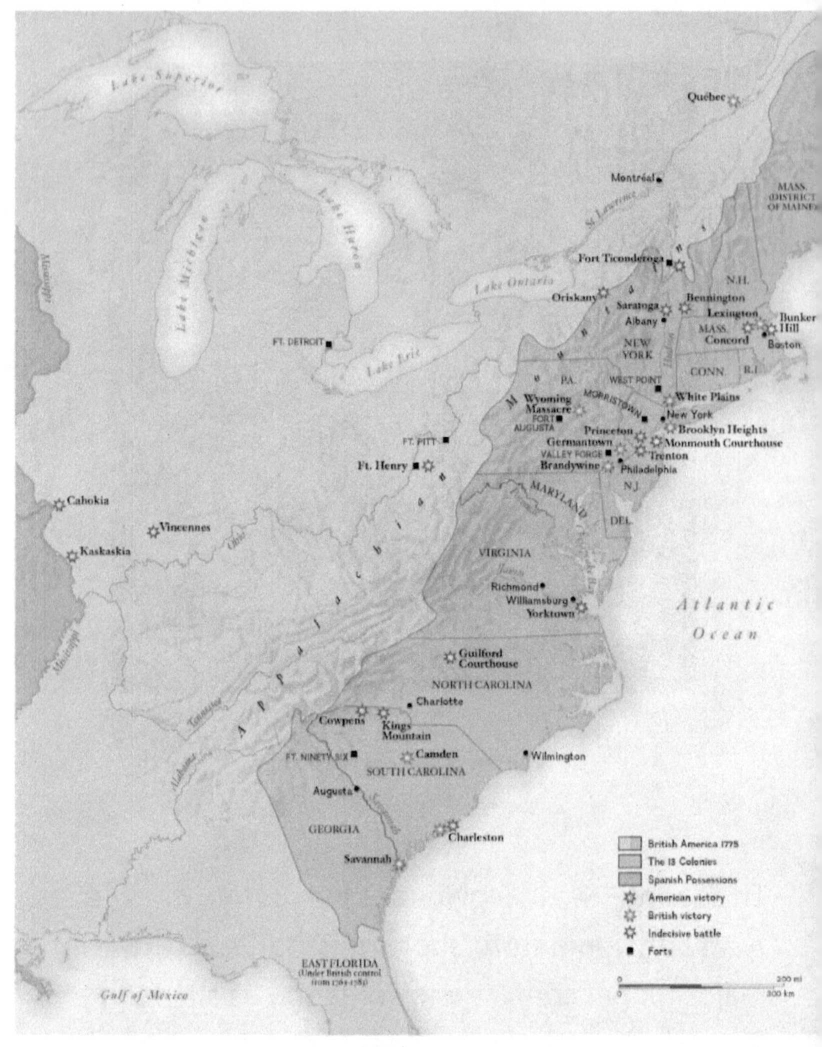

The above is a picture of the American colonies

Britian was victorius in this war and made some European powers concede, they also made France concede all of its territories in North America as a result of this. Britian later struggled with it's economy after this war and was in great debt, so, in order to combat this issue Britian later taxed the American colonies by imposing the acts such as the sugar act of 1764 which meant that the colonies had to import sugar exclusively from Britian and had to pay duties on it and there was also the infamous stamp act This act required colonists to pay tax on various forms of paper, documents and playing cards, represented by a government-issued stamp. This tax also applied to dice and newspapers.

The tax upset a lot of Americans, what made it even worse is that the Americans didn't have any representatives in the British Parliament that was issuing these taxes, as a result of this, many Americans protested by boycotting British goods and people who were found loyal to the British were increasingly harrased. The stamp act was so controversial that Britian had to repeal the stamp act a few years later. After this Britian still needed some income so they then made the declaratory act which stated that taxations in America were the same as in Britian, followed by this, they introduced the townshed acts which were a series of acts on taxes and regulations to the American colonies, due to this, the Americans boycotted British goods which led them to withdraw the act. The British sent 1000 troops to Boston to take control as the American perspective of the British at that time was terrible. This move raised the tension in Boston so much so that on march 5, 1770 a group of Americans started continuously throwing snowballs, rocks and sticks at a group of British soldiers guarding the customs house.

The British soldiers later lost their patience and shot at the crowd. Five civilians were killed and a news paper run by the American revolutionaries known as *"The Patriot press"* described this incident as a crime commited by the cruel British against the people of Boston. This incident enraged the people of Boston which made them against the British. After this, there were many more incidents which took place against the british for example, a revenue schooner was burned down by the locals and also when it was found out that the governor of Massachusetts was supporting the suppression of the colonists, his house was burned down by the locals and there was one famous and important incident on December 16, 1773 where a revolutionary group named *"The Sons of Liberty"* disguised as native American boarded a Bristish merchant ship in the Boston Harbour and in front of thousands of spectators threw thousands of pounds (£ British Currency) worth of tea overboard.

The British were outraged by this and punished the city of Massachusetts by dissolving its General Assembly, Revoking its charter and sending 3000 more troops to occupy the city. This move by Britian enraged the people of America. The other colonies had heard what was happening and were worried if they would be next so, they arranged a meeting (brains trust) where 56 delegates from the 12 colonies gathered and met in Philadelphia at the first Continental Congress on september 5, 1774 and decided to draft a formal petition about the colony's grievences to the British king at that time, King George III, the King did not accept this petition. After this, George washington ordered the local militias to start arming and be ready at a minute's notice. These "minutemen" stood ready for the beginning of the American revolutionary war.

Britain noticing this issue sent 700 troops under the command of General Thomas Gage to destroy the Patriots out in the rebel controlled Massachusetts countryside. Gage then planned to destroy the stock of arms and ammunition held by the Patriots in the city of Concord in the middle of the night. Paul Reveire, a patriot, warned the rebels that the British were coming which gave the Patriots time to prepare, the two forces eventually met in Lexington and faced off and in the confusion someone shot first. This was known as *"The shot heard around the world"* marking the beginning of the American war revolutionary war for independence, the battle had begun and the rebel forces were outnumbered and were pushed back by the British to Concord.

The British searched for rebel supplies meanwhile, the rebels were reinforced with more Patriots and were ready to push the British back, the British were then pushed back by the rebels and had to fall back to Boston, a humilating defeat for the Empire. when the British were retreating back to Boston they encountered rebel fire on the way and when they finally reached Boston, rebel militias surrounded them and Boston was put under siege. Small naval skirmishes would also continue in Boston

Later, trouble was starting to brew in New York when Col. Benedict Arnold planned a daring plan to take the British stronghold, Fort Ticonderoga which had a lot of supplies including arms and ammunition. Arnold then went on a journey to the fort, alone hoping to recruit some patriots along the way, he then came across a patriot group known as the *"Green Mountain boys"* led by Ethan Allen. Who had the exact plan as Arnold did so, with the Green Mountain Boys in charge the group raided the fort at night while the guards were sleeping and captured the fort and it's supplies with little to no resistance, another humiliating defeat for the British, due to the performance of General Gage in this war King George fired General Gage and replaced him with General William Howe and ordered him to put down the rebellion immediately.

The Continental Congress then made George Washington as the Commander- In- Chief of the Continental Army. Washington then began his journey to Boston to take control of the siege. The siege in Boston was about to take a turn when the British decided to plan an attack on Bunker hill, luckily, Continental spies were able to warn the army before the attack and the Continental army were able to set up defensive positions for an attack Bunker hill and nearby Breeds Hill and on 17 June, 1775 the day of the battle had arrived and when the British arrived they were met with Continental fire, they tried to advance up the hill twice and were pushed back twice, the Continentals had to retreat as they had run out of ammunition and the British were able to capture the hill.

The British suffered 1000 casualties while the continentals suffered 400 which showed that even when the British won the battle, they still managed to inflict losses onto them. For the remainder of the year small engagements continued between the colonies and Britian such as the burning of Falmouth, Massachusetts and Norfolk, the patriots managed to capitalise on this by using these as powerful propaganda tools and galvanising public opinion against the British.

The French and Spanish had an unpopular opinion of the British and so, they began supplying the Patriots, the Spanish did not officially enter the war. There were also disputes between Patriot and loyalist British militias in the colonies. Bendict Arnold, the person who recruited the green mountain boys, wanted to win some personal glory for himself so, he decided to invade parts of Canada by launching a two-pronged attack.

The Patriots managed to take Montreal and capture British soldiers there even though it was a difficult journey the Continentals managed to advance further to Quebec City, it was here however they would be pushed back all the way to Fort Ticonderoga due to harsh snowstorms and diseases during the expedition even though it was a failed expedition, it still managed to win Arnold some fame and respect. Speaking of fort Ticonderoga, Henry Knox, a patriot, had an idea for the arms and ammunition which were present there, he got together some oxen to transport the arms and ammunition all the way to Boston to help Washington and his army present there.

This helped boost the morale of the soldiers present there as now they could finally advance. Washington planned to launch a full-scale attack on the city but his soldiers warned him that the British were too well fortified and it could lead to a tremendous loss of life with no progression, thankfully, Washington was a somewhat openminded person at taking advices and later took the advice of his men. The new plan was to set up the artillery at Dorchester heights where the Continentals had an Advantage to fire artillery on the British. When dawn broke on March, 1776 the British knew they could not hold Boston at all, so, they began evacuating the troops in the in Boston at that time, this day was also known as evacuation day, 120 ships began evacuating 9000 redcoats and 2000 loyalists away to British occupied Canada.

Portrait of Henry Knox

This was the end of the siege of Boston, this victory boosted the morale of the soldiers and increased the support for the cause of the Patriots. There was also another important person who played a key role in the revolution, Thomas Payne, a writer, wrote two pamphlets which were "Common Sense" and "The American Crisis" in which he criticised monarchy and strongly advocated for American independence, these pamphlets were widely spread throughout the colonies.

In fact, George Washington found the first essay so inspiring that he ordered it to be read to his troops to boost their morale. Congress then began to consider the decision of Independence and so, Thomas Jefferson, an American revolutionary, was selected to write the official declaration of Independence and so, on the 4th of July 1776 the United States of America was formed. The war was still far from over, it took years for the war to end but on September 3, 1783 the American Revolutionary war was formally ended.

One more important event was when Benjamin Franklin, a patriot and a scientist, played a crucial role as he was sent to Paris to convince the French to join the war this would be important for our next topic,

2. The French Revolution

Before the French revolution France was divided into three social class which were the Clergy, Nobility and the commoners

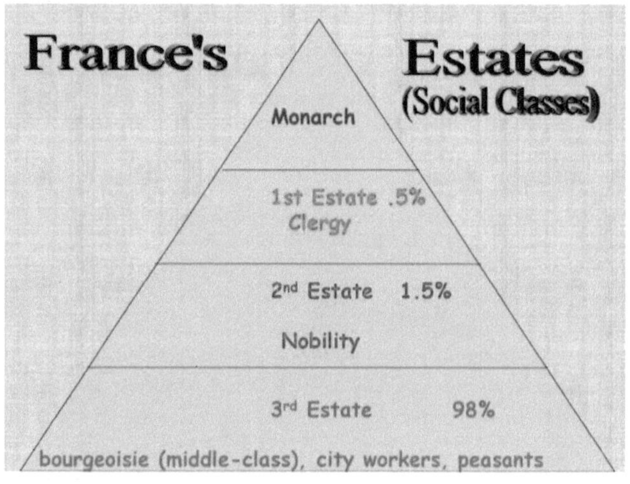

The first 2 estates enjoyed a life of privilege while the 3rd estate made up the majority, the common people of France. the royals would benefit off of the 3rd estate and would spend the money on their extravagant lifestyles. People In France began to question whether the nation was perfect and so, began the age of enlightenment where many philosophical thinkers in France questioned the authority of France, the separation of the church from power, it also played a strong emphasis on the rights of an individual and emphasised the importance of education. When king Louis XV died, Prince Louis Capet was dauphin (heir to the throne) and king of France on, May 10 1774, King Louis did not have the proper wisdom to rule France what was even worse was, France at this time was also going through an economic crisis. People around him such as court factions, financial ministers, etc, realised this and exploited him for their personal gain.

Portrait of King Louis

One of Louis' first acts was to get vengeance on the British for the 7 years' war by funding the American colonies' war for independence. France, had its vengeance but still, the victory costed them and France was in more economic ruin. The common people of France watched as

though the upper classes continued to live as if there was nothing wrong in the condition of France. The people of France continued to grow more disdainfully against their queen, Marie Antoinette who lived an extravagant life which earned her the nickname "*Madame Deficit*". (it's meaning implied that she had a lifestyle beyond revenue).

The people of France also ridiculed its monarchy through crude drawings. France was going through a financial crisis as mentioned earlier, so to combat this the king decided to tax the poor. The poor, already struggling to make ends meet, found themselves being taxed in every direction also, a huge portion of the peasants harvest had to be given up. There was even the labour tax where peasants had to work a certain number of days for their local lord without pay.

The tax rules were inconsistent throughout France and the nature of these private tax collectors were sometimes violent, on top of this, the first 2 estates found themselves to pay little to no tax. This raised the tension between the people of France. After these events a series of harsh summers and winters left the peasants harvest in ruin meaning there was a shortage of food and they now had no money because of the bad harvests, on top of this the cost of bread skyrocketed, which made it even worse for the people of France.

The upper class faced no problem with this crisis as they had massive stocks of food grain and wheat. *Remember Benjamin Franklin's diplomatic mission?* This inspired some people of France as it helped spread revolutionary ideas which took place in America but still, it did not influence the people of France directly.

The common people of France rioted, bakeries were raided and bakers suspected of keeping food for themselves were sometimes even hanged. Faced with this problem, King Louis decided to summon the estates general (a Legislative and consultative assembly made up of representatives of the three estates) it had not been summoned for over a century.

The two estates got one vote each, making sense as the population of them was less but, the third estate making up the large majority of the French population also got one vote. The third estate representing the vast majority of the population, demanded more influence and equal voting rights, arguing against the traditional voting by estate which gave disproportionate power to the 2 upper estates the clergy and nobility.

They soon realised that any attempt of reform they make can be voted out by the first two estates so, they decided to make an assembly known as the National assembly. King Louis noticing this ordered for them to be locked out of their meeting hall.

The National Assembly found a different hall nearby, a tennis court and its members then took "The Tennis Court oath" on 20th June 1789, pledging to continue meeting until the king gave into their demands for more equality, social and economic reform.

The national assembly was also made up of highly educated people of the 3rd estate such as Maximillian Robespierre and George Danton. Maximillian Robespierre went on to form a radical political party known as the Jacobin club or "the Society of the Friends of the constitution" George Danton and many others would go on to join this party even members of the first 2 estates would go on to join this party.

The Jacobins were different from others, where many just wanted reform, the Jacobins called for the removal of the king entirely. The king noticing everything going around in Paris ordered the military to take position around Paris. The National Assembly noticing this started to believe that the king was going to round them up and arrest them maybe, even execute them, not only this but, the king also dismissed France's popular finance minister, Jacques Neckar, who had been trying to make reforms himself. The people of France had decided they have had enough, the national assembly decided to announce the assembly of the *"bourgeois militia"* the National Guard, some members of the French military also defected to this side. On the 14th of July 1789, a large crowd stormed the Hôtel les Invalides (a military hospital) where they were able to secure some rifles.

In order to secure gunpowder for their rifles the crowd went near a prison fortress, a symbol of royal tyranny known as the Bastille. When the crowd was outside the Bastille, they demanded that the governor in charge, Governor De Launey, surrender the prison, release the prisoners and handover the gunpowder of the prison.

He initially refused and invited few members of the crowd for negotiation, this took a long time and the crowd lost their patience, the crowd stormed the fort taking on the French troops inside. Governor De Launey was captured and paraded through the streets of Paris, there were attempts to save him by a couple revolutionaries but the anger of the crowd made it difficult to do so. The National Assembly did not condemn this act and instead viewed it as a way of the people's frustration and anger towards the French Government, a heroic act of resistance and an important event of the revolution.

Portrait of the storming of the Bastille

Some historians also believe that this act paved the way for violence and bloodshed during the

French revolution. These acts could've also been inspired by the writings of a man of science, Jean Paul Marat, who had a skin condition which made him bedridden, it was perhaps this which made him interested in writing, Marat wrote in his radical newspaper named *"L' ami du peuple" or "The friend of the people"* in where he advocated for the poor, incited violence and used it for journalism and propaganda.

Portrait of Jean Paul Marat

After the storming of the Bastille the National Assembly wrote the "Declaration of the rights of man and citizen" with the help of *Thomas Jefferson*. Even with all this, the people of France were still struggling to make ends meets and blamed the king for his disconnection with the people since, the King lived in Versailles 20km south west of Paris and was separated from his subjects and lived in luxury.

On October 5th 1789, a crowd of 7000 women decided to march to the palace of Versailles to remove the separation and demand for reform, along the way many people followed them, eventually, they reached the Palace of Versailles and protested outside it, the protests got so violent that some members of the crowd broke in the palace with the intention of killing the queen.

They also managed to kill some of the royal guards inside. The queen then managed to escape out of a narrow passage in her bedroom. The King had no other choice but to go and address the crowd, he then agreed to share power with the revolutionary government and also agreed to return to Paris with the crowd thus, ending the separation between subject and king. With this, France started to shift towards a constitutional monarchy.

Now in the Tuileries Palace in Paris King Louis began to witness how the revolutionary government began to slowly strip away his power and implement their revolutionary ideas on to France and giving demands to the king such as one example, the tax money of France was used on the welfare of France and not on the King's lavish parties.

King Louis then decided to leave France and retake his country from abroad, this was possible for him due to Marie being an Austrian duchess so, on the night of June 20th 1791 the king and his wife disguised as servants headed for the

Picture of King Louis wearing the revolutionary bonnet

Austrian Netherlands but were caught by a postmaster in the town of Varennes and was sent back to Paris. The King's lack of support for the revolution was clear to the people of France, because of this, in the new constitution of 1791 the King was reduced to a simple figurehead and thus, France became a constitutional monarch however, radicals such as those in the Jacobin club were enraged that the king was not removed entirely.

They then staged a protest at the Champ De Mars on the 17th of July 1791 where they had a petition demanding to make France a republic, the government of Paris fearing an insurrection ordered the military to fire at the crowd.

This incident marked the division within the Brotherhood of the revolution with the two sides the Moderates wanting to keep the king as a figurehead on the other hand the radical who wanted the king to be deposed.

After the massacre the radicals managed to receive a wave of support. The revolution also introduced a new form of execution the

Guillotine, invented by Dr. Joseph Guillotine as a quick and painless way of execution instead of other previous inhumane executions anyone who was sentenced to this received it regardless of their social status, gender, economic status, etc. the writings of radicals such as, Marat and others suggested people to be executed such as, some people of the first two estates who benefited from the cruel system of inequality.

Local lords found their peasants rioting against them so most of them fled to other countries (émigré), the privilege classed of these foreign nations who were ruled by monarchs at the time feared that the revolutionary ideas that was spread through France would spread to their countries as well.

The National Assembly which was now the Legislative assembly feared that these countries might decide to attack due to several factors including the Declaration of Pill Nitz on august 1791 by Austria and Prussia issued by the Holy Roman Emperor Leopold II (Marie Antoinette's brother) which showed the willingness of the 2 countries to restore monarchy back to the throne. The Revolutionary Government felt threatened by this and declared war on Austria on April 1792, Prussia ended up joining the war alongside Austria.

During the war Another incident occurred where the Prussian duke of Brunswick wrote a letter to France stating that if anything happened to the king, he would burn Paris to the ground, this letter enraged the Parisians and raised the tensions in Paris so much so that on August 1792 a mob stormed King Louis' palace ending up killing some of the Swiss Royal guard who were protecting the King, King Louis managed to flee and take refuge in the Legislative assembly.

A vote was then held to suspend the monarchy entirely making France a republic and King Louis, Citizen Louis. Louis was then sent to prison where an eye could be kept on him. The Legislative assembly now, The National Convention officially declared the French republic on September 22, 1792. French society underwent massive changes, new enlightened ideas of democracy and equality were being implemented however, the new republic began to violently remove any semblance of the old regime. The Church was one of the targets of this, catholic priests who didn't take the revolutionary oath were either arrested or deported.

A new state sponsored atheistic religion began to emerge known as the *"cult of reason"* made as a replacement for the catholic church as a result of this, Notre Dame and many other churches had their religious treasures destroyed and were converted into temples of the cult of reason. The Christian calendar didn't survive instead a new "revolutionary calendar" was introduced. The government of Paris now under the control of the radical Sans-Culottes (lower class extreme revolutionaries) imprisoned whom they believed were "enemies of the revolution" and sending a large number of them to prison, most of them were members of the former upper estates.

As France's foreign enemies continued to close in, revolutionaries such as George Danton made impassionate calls for men to join the frontlines thousands of people from Paris went to join the frontlines in their absence, the people believed that the prisoners were spreading counterrevolutionary ideas against the government and if the enemies of France reached Paris and freed them, Marat believed that the former upper estates would enact their vengeance onto the people. With these beliefs. Fearing those whom they have already imprisoned the mobs stormed in Paris' prisons which resulted in the brutal *September massacres* where priests, aristocrats and others were tried and executed.

Women and children were not spared from this massacre. Over 1600 victims lost their lives in this. Word of the massacre spread across Europe the London Times wondered "Are these the rights of man? Is this the liberty of human nature?".

Maximillian Robespierre and his radicals wanted to see former king Louis on trial, since Austria and Prussia earlier declared that they would return Louis to the throne if they won. After this, Citizen Louis Capet was tried for treason and found guilty his punishment was decided by a vote whether to be deported or executed and by one vote Citizen Louis was sentenced to execution. *On the 21st of January 1793 Citizen Louis Capet was executed.*

Back on the frontlines, France started to push back Austria and Prussia but later more European countries joined in the coalition against France so, to combat this the National Convention introduced a new conscription law in which each regional department had to meet a certain quota for men to send to the frontlines but, outside of Paris many people somewhat disliked the revolution as they hated the violence the revolution brought with it and how anti-Christian it was now that they were being made to fight for the republic they despised, as a result of this, counterrevolutionary uprising took place in some parts of France some would go on to last for years.

An important incident took place in the French southern city of Toulon where the royalists of Toulon invited the British forced as well as its allies to stay and occupy the city, this being an important naval base served as a somewhat devastating blow to France. To break the siege, they sent some generals with their armies to break the siege one important incident in the army where a young naval officer by the name of *Napolean Bonaparte* presented a plan to some capture key fortifications in Toulon, his plan would be successful and for his actions he was promoted to Brigadier General, *he would go on to become one of the best military leaders of all time.*

Moving away from the frontlines, one pf the most significant counterrevolutionary uprisings took place in France's Vendee region the revolution saw brutal atrocities and brutal pacification committed by the military the infamous general that committed brutal atrocities in this region named Jean Baptist Carrier had an instance where he gathered men, women and children tied them to ships which ould then be sunk, he was later tried for war crimes, found guilty and executed.

Back in Paris, the economy was getting worse along with the counterrevolutionary uprisings the government and Marat had one scapegoat, the moderates, the Jacobins later declared an insurrection and called for the people to arm themselves, the moderate then ceased to be a political force through the arrest of 29 moderate Girondin politicians and the Legislative assembly started to be dominated by radicals.

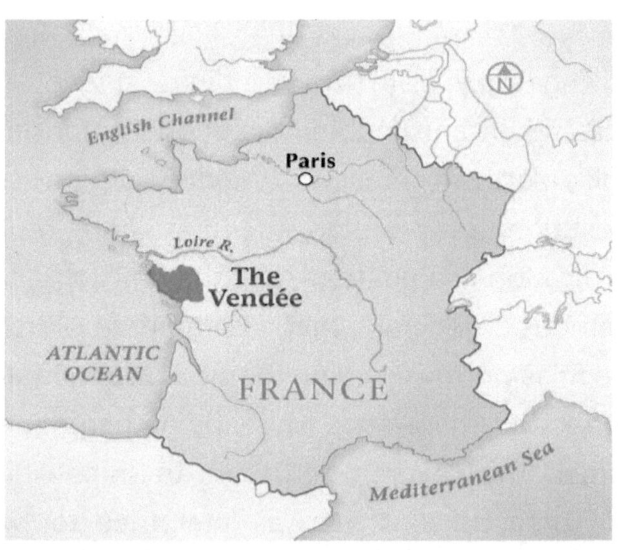

Away from Paris in the city of Caen was a woman named Charlotte Coday who was flabbergasted by how violent the revolution and the reason she believed the revolution was this violent was because of the writing of Marat. She then decided to go to Paris and inform Marat that she had a list of enemies for him to publish in his newspaper and ended up killing Marat on 13 July 1793.

She was later sentenced and Marat was martyred and in Temples of reason Marat symbols of the dead Marat were placed. After the death of Marat, a new period began known as *Reign of Terror* where there was a belief within the radical that there were internal enemies in France who conspired to take down revolutionary France and not loyal to the revolution so, to protect the people of France from suspected "enemies of the revolution two new institutions were established such as "the committee of public safety" and a new revolutionary tribunal where a special court was established to streamline the trials of France's internal enemies by execution.

On the September of 1793 it was declared in France that terror would be the new order of the day which started the *reign of terror.* Spies and secret police were everywhere watching the people to see if they would talk bad about the revolution. Many people were sentenced to execution because of this. More than 40000 people were executed as a result of this one of the most famous figures sent to the Guillotine was Marie Antoinette who was tried for treason, found guilty and later executed on 16th October 1793.

Things have finally gotten better for the French republic after this, the food situation improved and the French military was winning strategic battles. George Danton seeing this, talked to Robespierre about making some reforms, the two of them got into a conflict which made Robespierre charge Danton and his followers with charges of counterrevolutionary charges which had them sent to execution.

Robespierre also created a new religion known as the cult of the supreme being with its annual festival of the supreme being, Maximillian found himself slowly becoming mentally unstable his final mistake occurred on July 26 1794 giving a speech to the national convention defending his actions. The next day, Maximillian was arrested and his close followers were arrested too, Maximillian would later be executed. After the fall of Robespierre, a more moderate group known as the Thermidorians came into power and now, it was the radical themselves who were the target of political suppression.

Radical Sans Cullottees were the target of moderate Bourgeois street fighters during a period named *the White Terror.* The Thermidorians drafted a new constitution called the directory where they would try prevent power from falling into the hands of a single individual again. Monarchists used this opportunity to strike and Napolean Bonaparte was sent to take control of the crowd by firing on the insurrection, for his actions he was promoted to Napolean became a General and was sent to take control of the French armies in In Italy.

The new government of France was unpopular but as Napolean kept on winning more battles he became more popular with the French people. Long story short, he staged a coup against the Government and would later become the Emperor of France and make reforms to France. This was the end of the French revolution.

3. The Russian Revolution

In 19th century Europe, many countries were trying to implement the ideas of modernity such as, democracy, equality and liberty and inventing modern machines but, there was one country that stood from all, a country which at that time was backwards and what some might call medieval, Russia, ruled by Tsars still implemented serfdom and restricted had restricted rights on the citizens and a large portion of the population were serfs meaning they had to work for their landlords and could not even leave the land without permission of their landlords not only this, even education was reserved for the Russian Elite so, in simpler terms the poor were at a condition where they were kept poorer while the rich could get richer.

In 1861 Tsar Alexander II abolished serfdom but for the loss of free labour the serfs had to pay compensation to the landowners so, it placed some heavy burdens on the serfs but still, there were some benefits from this as serfs could now migrate to the cities and take up other work without their former landlord's permission but still, the people were dissatisfied about many things with the government. As a result of this, Tsar Alexander II was killed by a bomb thrown by a student called *I. Grinivitski* who was part of a revolutionary organisation known as *"The National will"*. After the death of Alexander II, Alexander III took his place as Tzar and felt that his father's reforms weakened the Tzars authority over the people and began oppressing on other ethnic minorities in Russia and began a policy of "Russification" where he wanted to unite the ethnic groups in Russia under one language and one culture under his reign antisemitic policies were also intensified.

When Tzar Alexander II he died of kidney inflammation, his son would take his place as Tzar his father failed to prepare him in his future role as Tzar. Nicholas himself admitted that he was not ready to be Tzar but, he still believed that he was chosen by God to do lead the nation and tried to lead Russia.

To boost his reputation with the people, Tzar Nicholas promised free food and drinks to a large crowd in Moscow however, due to improper planning, almost 1500 people died in this stampede. Tzar Alexander went to a party organised by the French, this tarnished his reputation severely.

Picture of Tsar Nicholas

The Russian people watched as the Tzars have been enjoying their privilege at the expense of the people for centuries and failed in giving the people rights whereas, the rest of Europe already started giving people rights. Many groups started to rise one group amongst them lead by Vladimir Ilyich Ulyanov or Vladimir Lenin a rebellious man who was once expelled from his university for participating in a student protest, him and his group were led by an idea which was called Communism which was from Karl Marx's teachings in his manifesto. Communism is an ideology where there are no social class divides, workers weren't exploited and had more rights and everyone is equal. Karl Marx taught in his manifesto that capitalism was made to exploit the workers and the workers could only get rid of it through a revolution.

Lenin read that manifesto and believed in its ideas. Since Lenin did not believe in the Tsar's autocratic rule he was exiled to Siberia where he would write socialist newspapers. After his exile, he moved to western Europe where he could express his adoration for communism and was free to discuss with other Marxists.

Lenin then joined a party with other Russian communists and many people in the party disagreed with Lenin's beliefs so much so, that Lenin caused a split in the party with 2 sides the Bolsheviks on Lenin's side and the Mensheviks those who were in opposition to Lenin (Bolshevik means majority while Menshevik meant minority) the Bolsheviks were in the minority and the Mensheviks were in the majority. Lenin would still write socialist newspapers which would then be smuggled into Russia in hopes of influencing the people towards Communism.

The Mensheviks were less radical while Lenin demanded loyalty from his men towards his uncompromising ideas. The Mensheviks also feared that Lenin's attitude could lead to a dictatorship.

Picture of Lenin

Lenin waited for an opportunity to overthrow the Tsar and continued to write socialist newspapers. Back in Russia, one of the Tsar's most skilled advisors Sergei Witte, wanted to modernise Russia and convinced Tsar Nicholas who later agreed to it. He then built factories in Russia through foreign Capital. The workers of the factories had to work long hours in terrible conditions and were paid less.

To combat this, the workers went on a strike. The tension in Russia rose as the workers wanted better working conditions, liberals wanted reform and the peasants wanted rights, there was one solution, war, there was an opportunity for war in the far east when Russia wanted to expand its sphere of influence toward northern China (the Manchuria region) where Japan wanted to do it too.

The emperor of Japan at that time Emperor Meiji proposed an idea by reducing the tension by not interfering the Russians in Manchuria if they didn't interfere the Japanese in Korea, the Russians refused. The Tsar then declared war on Japan. Tsar Alexander thought Japan could've been easily invaded but failed to realise as Japan had been rapidly militarising over the years so, when the Japanese launched a surprise attack on the fleet of port Arthur the Russians were shocked and later ended up starting to lose the war.

Russians were overjoyed with patriotism until Russia was losing the war. Upon hearing the defeat, the Russian people were outraged and the tensions in Russia increased. It would only take one more incident for the first revolution to start. On January 1905 when an orthodox priest named Father Gapon marched to the winter palace (where the Tsar lived) with his followers in a peaceful protest with a petition with a list of suggestions for the Tsar to improve the people's lives. The Tsar left a few days ago and in his place many troops arrived. Father Gapon and his followers were shot down in the protest.

Nicholas didn't personally give the orders to fire on them but since he was the Tsar, a complete autocrat, he was believed to have ordered them to fire. This event became known as *Bloody Sunday*. There were strikes across the empire not only this, the sailors in the Russian Navy started to mutiny, the tensions in Russia rose, this signified the beginning of the 1905 revolution.

New elected local councils called "Soviets" came into play, these Soviets consisted of Marxists. These Soviets coordinated strikes and supplied the workers. There were many different people who were on a strike in the empire, one among them were liberals who wanted more freedom. To please this group, Tsar Nicholas agreed to share power with them in a new constitution. He also agreed to have his was approved by an elective assembly called the duma. Tsar Nicholas ended the war with Japan and brought the troops back home, with the troops back home, Tsar Nicholas was able to put down the strikes and this is the conclusion of the 1905 revolution.

Tsar Nicholas still continued his autocratic rule and did not require his laws to be approved by the duma. Lenin still in western Europe tried to radicalise the people with socialist newspapers but couldn't complete this task at that time. he then started to believe that the only way Russia could succeed was through an armed revolution by the workers.

Back in Russia, after the 1905 revolution the Tsar got himself, a new advisor named, Pyotr Stolypin, who cracked down with more intensity than his predecessor so much so, that thousands of people were sentenced to death, this event earned itself a nickname called *Stolypin's necktie.*

Many positive reforms were still made and the Russian economy was starting to get back on its feet. Lenin watching this felt that he couldn't start a revolution in Russia at the moment so he had to wait. Back in Russia, a man named Rasputin was getting popular for his supernatural ways of treating his patients.

The Tsar noticing this decided in 1906, to ask Rasputin to treat his son, the Tsarevich of Russia, Alexei, who was suffering from haemophilia. Rasputin managed to treat his son possibly by taking the Tsarevich of his prescribed aspirin.

After this act, Rasputin became close to the royal family, which ruined the royal family's reputation as Rasputin himself had a terrible reputation and was believed to be mentally unstable. The press were initially banned from reporting on Rasputin but after sometime the ban was lifted and it spread among the people and the story became a scandal.

As the economy was improving and Russia was stable at this time the story wasn't an issue until, long story short, a man named Gavrilo Princip who worked for a Serbian secret society assassinated Archduke Franz Ferdinand of Austria-Hungary, Austria-Hungary sent a list of demands to Serbia which Serbia didn't accept them all so Austria-Hungary declared war on Serbia, Serbia's allies including Russia joined in the war and Austria's allies also joined in this war, this war became known as *World War 1* and now we shall continue from here.

The Russian people were filled with patriotism so much so, the renamed St. Petersburg to Petrograd as St. Petersburg sounded too German. The Russian army was outdated and hence, faced defeat after defeat although the soldiers were patriotic and would prove to go to defend their motherland at any cost, they were faced with many problems some of them even deserted the battlefields.

Tsar Nicholas would later make himself as the commander of chief of the army and would make his German wife take charge of the country. Russia was fighting against the Germans and when Tsar Alexander's German wife was in control of Russia the people did not find this well, on top of this, Rasputin lived with the royal family and this was an even worse look for the family. Seeing this, a group of Russian nobles decided to assassinate Rasputin, his death is somewhat shrouded in mystery and speculation to this day.

The war had been taking a large toll on Russia's resources most worryingly food, the people got hungry so, on March 8th 1917, International Women's Day, a crowd of women gathered to protest and wanted the Tsar to abdicate, the next day, the men joined them too, even the troops who were supposed to put down the riots sided with the protesters and thousands of soldiers mutinied in the capital, destroying symbols of the Tsar and his regime. The Liberals watched and they too had been dissatisfied with the Tsar the tensions in the city rose high.

Nichola got on a train to Petrograd, his train was met by generals midway and the generals forced him to abdicate. After the Tsar abdicated no one in the Romanov family was interested in ruling Russia and this was the end of Romanov rule in Russia. After the Tsar's death, The Duma set up the provisional government and became the official government while the "soviets" made up of Mensheviks and social revolutionaries gave orders to the workers and soldiers. The Germans realising an opportunity to strike directly at the heart of Russia sent Lenin on a train to possibly stir up tension in Russia. Lenin, upon hearing the things that had been occurring in Russia mentioned in his April thesis how he disliked the provisional government.

The Provisional Government even with its disadvantages was still appreciated by the people for its reforms such as the dismantlement of the secret police, the abolishment of the death penalty and plans of elections. To get the support of the people Lenin and the Bolsheviks invented a new slogan which was *Peace Land Bread* this slogan meant that they would end the war, ensure peace, provide people with land and food.

Lenin also called for all power to the soviets which meant to dissolve the provisional government and let the soviets' rule. Due to these slogans The Bolsheviks became more popular among the people and even some Mensheviks defected to their side. The war turned bad for Russia as failed offences took a heavy toll on the Russian economy.

Due to these reasons violent riots took place in Petrograd, the Bolsheviks tried to distance themselves from the violence but the people protested using Bolshevik slogans. On July 16-20 1917 came a period known as the *July Days* where workers and soldiers staged armed demonstration against the provisional government.

These protests were violently put down by the minister of war, Alexander Kerensky. Kerensky, now the Prime Minister, watching the protests by the people using Bolsheviks slogans, decided to step down on the Bolsheviks. Bolshevik leaders were imprisoned and Lenin was accused of being a German agent and had to flee to Finland in disguise.

The Bolshevik protests had upset the Liberals and factory owners so, in order to please them Kerensky decided to promote famed General

Kornilov to the supreme commander of the Russian armed forces. Kornilov was a devout anti socialist and despised the new socialist reforms of the government, he then ordered his soldiers towards Petrograd to dismantle the soviets. Kerensky hearing this freed the Bolshevik leaders, including a Bolshevik leader named Ivan Trotsky who would be pivotal in the defence of Petrograd where he ordered the workers to sabotage Kornilov's advancements.

The workers sabotaged Kornilov's advancement by diverting his trains, sabotaging his communication and even some workers managed to convince the demoralised troops to desert. A large majority of the workers were also armed but, eventually Kornilov's coup fell apart and he ended up being arrested. This whole incident became beneficious for the Bolsheviks as they grew more in popularity and were elected to the Petrograd Moscow Soviets with Trotsky as its chairman.

This meant they were in a very powerful position and Lenin could return back to Petrograd and start the Communist revolution. The Bolsheviks then began to plan the revolution and some members argued against this and stated that it was too violent and wrote news articles about this. Kerensky, hearing this began arresting Bolsheviks and the Bolsheviks felt that they had to commence the revolution immediately so, on 8th march 1917, the Bolshevik revolution commenced. With Lenin in hiding, Trotsky organised the Bolshevik militia and later took control of the city and Kerensky escaped before the Bolshevik militia was now about to take control of the winter palace. With the Winter Palace in siege, Lenin came out of hiding to play a bigger role in the revolution, with no resistance the Bolshevik militia took control of the winter palace, arrested the provisional government and took control of Russia.

The new government then held elections in which the Bolsheviks lost. Lenin seeing this shut down their assembly and took control of the government again. The people protested and the protests were put down violently. The Bolsheviks also began to set up secret police in response to this, an attempt on Lenin's life by Socialist Revolutionary Party Member (the party which was in power but Lenin seized it) Fanny Kaplan in which Lenin was seriously wounded. In response, the Bolsheviks began cracking down on counterrevolutionary suspects. Back on the frontlines, Lenin had promised peace so, Lenin then made Trotsky commissar for foreign affairs, Trotsky used this role to negotiate a peace deal with the Germans.

The Germans then drafted a peace treaty in which Trotsky had an idea with what called "*No war no peace*" in which he would not sign the treaty and would not order any offences.

Picture of the treaty

The Germans taking advantage of this pushed deep into Russian territory which then prompted another peace treaty with even harsher terms.

This treaty was devastating to the Russian economy but still, Russia didn't have to fight the war anymore which meant the Government could focus on developing the country. Many reforms were made during the Russian revolution such as the reforms, Peace, Land and bread. Russia would go on to face many more challenges such as civil war between the Tsarist whites and the communist red where brutal atrocities were committed on both sides and in the end the Communist reds won and implemented the idea of Communism that the Russians had of classlessness and complete equality and this revolution would lay down the foundation of the Union of Soviet Socialist Republics or the Soviet Union.

This revolution would go on to inspire many more communist revolutions around the world and this is where we will conclude.

4. Image Sources

Wikipedia

History Net

History Extra

Epilogue

The American, French, and Russian revolutions are more than just events in history; they are examples of how people can bring about significant change. Each of these revolutions started because people were unhappy with the way things were and wanted something better. They believed in the power of standing up for their rights, and their efforts shaped the world we live in today.

The American Revolution led to the creation of the United States, a country built on the principles of freedom and democracy. The French Revolution sparked new ideas about human rights and equality, ideas that would go on to become the building blocks of democracy. The Russian Revolution brought dramatic changes to politics and society, introducing communism and creating a new kind of government.

Even though these revolutions took place a long time ago, their impact is still felt today. We can learn from these moments in history and use their lessons to improve our world. Whether it's fighting for justice, equality, or freedom, revolutions remind us that people have the power to create change when they work together for a common cause.

www.ingramcontent.com/pod-product-compliance
Lightning Source LLC
LaVergne TN
LVHW091228150826
845673LV00003B/1058

* 9 7 9 8 8 9 6 1 0 0 9 7 3 *